CHIMPANZEES

by Liza Jacobs

BLACKBIRCH®
PRESS

THOMSON

GALE

San Diego • Detroit • New York • San Francisco • Cleveland • New Haven, Conn. • Waterville, Maine • London • Munich

For more information, contact
The Gale Group, Inc.
27500 Drake Rd.
Farmington Hills, MI 48331-3535
Or you can visit our Internet site at http://www.gale.com

Photographs © 1991 by Chang Yi-Wen

Cover Photograph © Tim Davis/CORBIS

© 1991 by Chin-Chin Publications Ltd.

No. 274-1, Sec.1 Ho-Ping E. Rd., Taipei, Taiwan, R.O.C.
Tel: 886-2-2363-3486 Fax: 886-2-2363-6081

LIBRARY OF CONGRESS CATALOGING-IN-PUBLICATION DATA

Jacobs, Liza.
  Chimpanzees / by Liza Jacobs.
    v. cm. -- (Wild wild world)
Includes bibliographical references (p. 24).
Contents: Primates -- Grooming -- Food -- Smart Tool Makers -- Baby Chimps.
  ISBN 1-4103-0031-5 (hardback : alk. paper)
  1. Chimpanzees--Juvenile literature. [1. Chimpanzees.] I. Title. II. Series.

QL737.P96J229 2003
599.885--dc21

2002154166

Printed in Taiwan
10 9 8 7 6 5 4 3 2 1

Table of Contents

Primates

Chimpanzees live in the forests and grasslands of Africa.

They are apes and belong to a group of animals called primates. Apes, monkeys, and humans are all primates. Primates have large brains and are intelligent.

Male chimpanzees are between 4 and 5 feet tall and weigh 100 to 175 pounds. Females are a little smaller than males. Unlike monkeys, apes have no tails.

A chimpanzee's arms are longer than its legs. Chimpanzees usually walk on all fours.

Social Creatures

Chimps are very social animals. They love to play and take good care of each other.

Mothers protect and nurse their babies. Older children sometimes help their mother take care of younger children.

Napping and Nesting

Chimpanzees often take naps in the afternoon and sleep again at night.

In the wild, they make nighttime nests. It only takes a few minutes for a chimpanzee to make a cozy nest in the trees. It bends branches and twigs to make a platform and then softens it with leaves.

A chimpanzee sleeps alone, unless it is a mother. A mother chimp shares her nest with her baby.

A Swinging Life

Chimpanzee bodies are made for climbing and swinging in trees. Their arms and hands are very strong.

Chimps have hands that can easily hold on to things. A chimpanzee's feet and hands have thumbs for grasping branches.

This baby chimp is learning how to climb and swing while playing.

Communities and Parties

Chimps live together in groups called communities. A community can be as many as 100 chimpanzees. Within a community, smaller groups gather called parties.

A party roams the forest together. They use their sharp senses of smell, hearing, and eyesight to look for food and stay out of danger.

Parties are made up of a few females and their young, as well as one or more males. A party can also be just a few males.

At night, the whole community often gathers again, to sleep in trees near each other.

Chimps within a community rarely fight. But they will defend their territory from chimps in other communities.

Grooming

Chimpanzees spend time grooming, or cleaning, themselves each day.

They use their lips and fingers to comb their fur and get rid of dirt, bugs, and dead skin. Chimpanzees do this to stay calm as well as keep clean. They also groom each other to show affection.

A group grooming session can go on for hours!

Food

Chimps spend most of their waking hours either looking for food or eating it. They eat leaves, seeds, flowers, nuts, and bark. Chimpanzees also like honey, insects, and eggs. Sometimes they hunt for meat.

One of a chimpanzee's favorite foods is fruit. When a chimp comes across a tree full of ripe fruit, it is happy to share. The chimp will swing from the tree and make loud hooting noises to call others to the feast.

Smart Tool Makers

These intelligent animals are good at solving problems. They even make tools.

Chimpanzees enjoy eating termites. But termites live inside hard mounds.

A chimp will find a stiff stem or twig and strip off the leaves with its teeth. Then it will use the twig to poke inside a termite mound. The termites bite the twig and the chimp pulls out its lunch!

Chimps also use tools such as rocks to break open nuts. They use leaves to soak up water to drink or to wipe their hands after eating.

Chimps teach their tool-using skills to their young.

Baby Chimps

Chimpanzees can mate at any time of the year.

A mother is pregnant with her baby for about 8 months.

A baby chimp weighs about 4 pounds and depends upon its mother to survive.

The mother always keeps her baby with her, carrying it on her back or under her stomach.

The baby will nurse for the first 4 or 5 years of its life. It also eats some solid food by 6 months old. By 7 or 8 years old, it is ready to leave its mother.

Baby chimps love to play! And all the chimps in a community like to play with the babies.

Chimp Talk

Chimps communicate by using more than 30 sounds.

Chimps scream, whimper, grunt, bark, and make a pant-hoot noise.

Every chimp sounds different. Chimpanzees can tell each other apart by their voices.

Chimps also express themselves with their bodies and faces.

They hug, kiss, and hold hands. They can look and act happy, sad, angry, excited, and nervous.

These special
animals are
more like people
than any other
living creature.

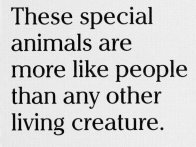

For More Information

Donovan, Sandra. *Chimpanzees.*
Austin, TX: Raintree Steck-
Vaughn, 2002.

Fink Martin, Patricia A. *Chimpanzees.*
Danbury, CT: Childrens Press,
2000.

Greenburg, Dan. *Chimpanzees.* New
York: Marshall Cavendish, 2001.

Glossary

community a large group of
chimpanzees

nest a chimpanzee's bed

party a small group of chimpanzees
within a community